IT'S NO WONDER MANY BIRDS ARE

THE SIZE OF A HUMAN HEART

LANCE PHILLIPS

AHSAHTA PRESS
THE NEW SERIES

MIMER

#66

BOISE, IDAHO 2015

Ahsahta Press, Boise State University, Boise, Idaho 83725-1525
ahsahtapress.org
Cover design by Quemadura
Book design by Janet Holmes

LIBRARY OF CONGRESS CATALOGING-IN-PUBLICATION DATA

Phillips, Lance, 1970–
[Poems. Selections]
Mimer / Lance Phillips.
pages ; cm.—(The new series ; #66)
ISBN 978-1-934103-56-2 (softcover : acid-free paper)
ISBN 1-934103-56-X (softcover : acid-free paper)
I. Title.
PS3616.H46A6 2015
811'.6—dc23
2014034765

FOR KELLY, ALWAYS

CONTENTS

MIMER

Each word he used was a mouthful and a butterfly so he feigned muteness and consulted his graph. The graph tacked there on the ceiling was easily mistaken, misjudged, for a map of some island, well traveled though not well populated--a misjudgment he did not correct.

The scar was an A. The screw from a bicycle horn tore back his skin in this shape, revealing the fat. Blood was surprisingly scarce. Stooping, picking up a red scarf, finding snow beneath. The apex of the A is directed hence from his heart.

A broken then mended digit foretold the illusory, crow, crow, tree frogs, a rhetorician's heart which on elucidation left crow out of crown.

The shape blood assumes when absorbed or diluted cannot be ignored:

lips on a tissue, a bird in the toilet water.

A mark on the graph was as good as something bartered.

Ever knowing all peripheries, the thighs are a Tiresias of the body proper.

He'd never thought his feet such an engine for arousal. Bodies
have the effect of so many prophets to him: a gesture as
simple as lifting a hand to remove a hangnail with the teeth
was a whirlwind or a whale. There is motion in any occupied
space and that motion, by turns, is egregious and absolutely
miraculous.

He pointed, and with a motion of his chin filled the entirety of expectation as a wind. The proper description of the place, any place—a wall, for instance, whether plaster or gypsum—has the authority of a polyp relegated to the dark labyrinthine enclosure of the throat or intestines. There are seven virgins at every turn, so that satiety is as good as pocketed.

The shape of his voyeurism concedes too many things and situations; it is rather animal in nature and highly adaptable. The ladder remains an object of affection for him even throughout its purpose. This tendency is borne out as he moves down the ladder and closes the window like feeding a child with his fingers.

There were days when the pressure of coincidence would weigh with such heft at the base of his skull that he seemed not to retrieve shapes in a normative manner. It was not unlike a seduction in which caring would be the diverted path, the call, along which bodies would remain useless until someone flinched, then, rushing back, would assemble and the quick stifle of mistake would chirrup back into what was then the sparrow in the holly just out the window.

Through description, his body, which always seemed borrowed, worked as if by stepping through a certain threshold or into a particular light: all would fall away leaving nothing like spirit but objects convoluted with that thinking which constructs passion and desire. The grasp on a pine cone differs in degree only from the grasp on his penis; the renditions of this grasp are of course numerous and self-indulgent. He assembled a small circle of thoughts about this and, not without irony, thought it the spirit of his age.

The dahlias were surely beautiful as were their measurements and descriptions.

Wouldn't measuring, with index finger and thumb, the slight wall between the anal cavity and the vaginal cavity of a woman require a more fixed and intimate understanding of not only the body, but possibly the methods one has of imagining space? Circling this line of thought down to a moment of establishment in the ear ever so long ago would have the effect of a cold towel on him as he sits with legs and arms crossed, breast folded into knees so that making himself small would in turn enlarge everything which is not him.

To muster a guard against iconoclasm he would follow a moth's curved abdomen as a beacon at head level around the room approaching and retreating from the light, the windows, even the mirror in which he, each time, found his glare arresting. The moth brought with it a device akin to that of the chorus in a Greek play, the level-headed commentator or the judge, whichever it was, in those fevered steps, that chase; the doing replicated a population and he a city which it inhabited.

There was, for him, concentric solitude; it was concise, solid and useful as a tooth. There was also linear solitude which, through the introduction of Time, was rather like bleeding.

The body heals, caught up in preservation, and the events are transformed into the story of the events so that a tooth or the skin of the skull adapt accordingly and can stand instead for any of us.

It's no wonder many birds are the size of a human heart.

What if on this occasion he were to take his face as the expression of something other than his intent?   A scowl: that knot of spiderlings. Grinning: a rough handling. Perplexity: something, an unspeakably soft and warm wound brought about through unbridled desire plus tow-headedness, winsome hand cupped under an apple. The rhinoceros, the monkey, and the camel have been written over by the opportunity to furrow his brow.

The problem, ultimately, is in what he takes for his body. There was this sense of taking the day into his mouth, as a smooth stone, of tucking it under his tongue so that by mimicking speech in this way it was fully occluded, an angry sun and its carnage, which he'd spend the remainder of time before dark renaming: thyroid, trachea, branching artery, sloop among the bile and distance to pass through.

He was dumbfounded at the minutiae, at the sheer will of that process which seemed to force his hand with regard to the graph. Primus, he could call his mind there in the diffuse light. Primus, which painted the walls and added grain to the floorboards; Primus, the sense made of the marks on the graph, the sense of imagining to speak; Primus, whatever animal heart was a scourge to him in his socks and deep in memory. Goose-pimples all the while he was repositioning the graph on the ceiling and all the while he wrote *Primus* over the outline of his body as a continuous barrier, dipping and rising in small letters and touching the horizon of skin just as a hand in the sea.

Consequence was kept at arm's length by the quick succession
of changes, by the need for these changes and the need to record
them. Deep within the vistas he'd brought up with a nearly
cellular clarity, which was in itself dazzling, the slick coat of
the nerves was thinning so that his muscles were not his own.
One can see in an object or an event the spiral it carries close
to it which is a matter of information organized in such a way,
into the head of a medicinal flower celebrated for its scarcity
for instance which when placed just so in the mouth of a dead
weasel by its mate has the effect of resurrection. This graph
carried within it, though unencumbered, the opposition of
contingency.

Somebody in some action placed a clipped notion of regalia, as the scent of a musk, into him. Thoughts were becoming so many adornments woven among a context as a wren might weave one of his hairs among the pine straw and twigs of her nest. Placing things usurped the things themselves as necessary. To this end the day was embraced, called forth as if, by his acceptance, diurnal life could begin each morning; the warmth from which he arose became his bed; what struck at his eyes in the harsh, interloping light, the room around, the window. The sense of power achieved through such meandering was dizzying, though behind it all and not totally without his acknowledgment, there was laughter from the street the cause of which was hidden from him. The face of god, for all he knew, had been evidenced, recorded in the asphalt or in the shape of a woman's skirt blown up by a morning breeze or in the laugh itself, confident and bright and called upon so as to disarm. The sun dragged with it the sleep of habit and lack of concern; pins and needles enveloped his left arm as he squeezed it into his chest.

SUB-

THE HUMAN IS OVER

Semen & mint from the basin

One indicates eye with grinding teeth, sun

Can see about blue sky that pear and drab resist

Lick and rain comes at right angles to the window

The wind, a face as a prod

Two fingers laid across the eyes, lyingly added

In a sense her movement is nothing other than the real

The crickets being something closer than the wall

One thinks a tree or sees a tree and has tree in the text, tree of
    predictables

Despising that leaf sense composes a toad, a sound she carries with her her sound, pitted right nipple

Virgil the news one has a mind
It can see you you it Venus still

Block a moral block distending
House into his ship and men
For describe gum-ridge white
While crying discomfort for
Herself leaf sea

Eventualities honeycomb out mouth
Besieged have am silver sill peck
Under curtain moon propriety
Moan his ear due again
Moan shriller value a one
Must simply accept as to money
The world below Sybil tearing
A squash an apple beating her
Breast before him marked domicile

Dove scruffs itself round
Mourning actual the plant
Name really there creeping
Thyme adage upon death
Of personage until bones shone
His eardrum with puss shone
White publicly prostitute
Touch is a vision to exceed
Thumb within thinking labial
Surface these earthy red leaves

Ginger molasses what one puts into
Remains wind sleeve over around
Sleeve dejecta one says the shade
Shadow hooks from quickly could
Intend chair over cheek eye brunt
Of weight boat bears Sibyl nuts
And a few berries automatic motion
What intent berryeye could push
Through its skin at what point
Do the dead fulfill their objects

The acquires ridiculously window
Perfect slip creased arm into torso
Bios crack one can Avernus
Each Hades pectoral deltoid so
Obviously helplessness rises black
Morning a sleep one can fold from
The hair mouth as bronze as substance
Over breast clear across one thinks his
Thinking profane laps the water

Theseus the mark riven into
Apple firm horror joy Hippolytus
For January night indelibly one
Expends energy all moon two
To have done with the limbs
Each tree horror traced one cannot
Help but describe and so snuff
Into Pleiades slight
Seven flesh ridges a texture black
Morning desire horror joy raise
One finger wrapped with her
Hair   list

Lists

Order cling and pivot woodpecker
Falls to sequence parasitic
Foregrounds each ovoid tooth lip
Stretch sweet any number within
The room tar paper and sugar

These holes jay blue black then white
Barred fifty mouths Hydra the trees
Figuration does information have a past
Each circle lineage composed of radii
Snow one can taste musk and body flees
Flees a boundary as what happens beyond
That gate she is privy to breast taken
From mouth January 12 cold dry
Dawn flag

Flag

That opportunity wheels through topic
Sheet water earth of forgetting down
To lip tongue crows with bread belly
Distended what I took so often as a face
Those lesions eyes legion talk one has
The night house talk the house trickle
Talk into windows squirrels talk distends
Surface

Torn from paper fist valves of heart
Sleep against lips appellation once future
Appellation come with basket a weave from
Supper itself crease a wonder the vernix
Yellow slight wind already the women
Voice concern these are enough futures
Well formed before you one perpetuates
This

2 jays

FROM NIETZSCHE'S BED

Legs by private list   wren culls iris

One moves one's foot by convulsion of Nature.   One insists
on the lamp.   How can one convalesce with the birds
singing to her?   Draw tree limbs with timelines.   One
believes the cold to be word of mouth.

Nostril produces the nouns
divided from themselves: pearl
the summer sky, happening

Digs throat through liriope doe rabbit

Smile yes toad The red inside fennel stalk from Prometheus

**struck dumb
**winter apples
**slowly those motions from tree to mouth approaching
**gag
**forced the field

Figuration: fly's leg for scale, groping finger

Method: spider
Constraint: laced into pear tree's crotch

By lips, lips by moon lit

At the setting: jaw.

Lashing accomplishes, by waves, mimic; pulps; spat; spat to
hone into him honeyed-apricot eye

One assumes bodily intervening through the room disportraiture
soft on the lips

Missive bird rides upon one.

The analogy one believes the snow
makes bird the extreme love
Know that dirt, that academy

" . . . yes, with proper technique and patience, the upholstery tack could *be* both Troy and Calypso's nipple . . ."

Brilliant one finds the mouth to it and through adjustment the object itself.

Does one *make*: "hand in the night, against concision, sweat under the baby's head"

Having seen nothing for two days my eyes are diffuse over the
coverlet.

Little bird: against description she moved within her circle of perception; her glass globe; her own skin, warmer in place of others.
Little bird: she takes horror to mean an emotive description.
Little bird: so that she removes her capacity to grasp by removing her hands.
Little bird: none.

Toad's back broke

Regard the proposition wet grass

Had taken the cage filled with singing birds and butchered each, with an eye toward portraiture.

One can say opal until one's tongue swells.

One hawk may not mean the mouth at risk.

The narrative pattern should cause schism between its components. For example if one says "sun" a receptacle primed with touch and lick must not only be warmed, become dappled and sweat, but ought to assume the aspect of being seen.

There's bluebird to think porch from idle

Button-jar as good as, come and see the third person stop
in me

The stances are parodies thus far; gorgon-headed and the like.

Project of a thought pales.

Only pre-established are their bodies, head finally turned on them.

Gentle one repeats. Gentle form for grief.

ANONYMITY

As purveyor Eros kept a thimble embossed with eyes.

A fashioner of trinkets from his body: the liminal hand, skull, squirrel.

Trickery gathers, forming his hand.

One stroke into wren
Retaining the act or victim
Cupped from recognitions
The prospects: hand+sun

Depicting includes:
consort
ants, winged, lain double
welts raise this shape across her back

*"Do you see this shape?" one makes one's own hand Crucible into
which goes spit.*

Gathers her hair
    Removed their substance then facing a tempest the twelve ships
    One remembers with centipede under heel at pre-dawn, crush
    The crushing wind
into a column within his fist.

One has honeyed-eye, in icon's stead, honed

Her feet, perched on biceps

Counterfactuals: largely the spider blown

One's resolve, rightly, enters cicada humming the downspout

One splits grapes upon one's palate for her

One has them wet, chronological, from her mouth
Almonds fall over sink into hand

Sun describes smaller, firmer moth larvae
"We must curl them thus like platelets and distribute them thus
beneath the tree for the ants to mob."

(i) Bad or ugly things: into its abdomen curled

(ii) Negatives: yellowjacket

(iii) Transitory things: flesh pressured into

(iv) Parts: intimate

(v) Accidents: sincerely

(vi) Composites: grip

(vii) Things which come to be from heterogeneous
combinations: sun

(viii) Acts depending on human will or resulting from
concatenation of many
causes: soon

Asters share with gigantism,
as though food for the dead

was

white aster,

1. crosses her face tactilely, entirely the spider
2. future one has as Cerberus
2a. to move one engages, even as Hercules, each head
chronologically

Bid

redundancy right arm links
elbow palm backward cupped
fingers Harpies would say
splayed

Blue

mostly this, Atlas
upon the maple
the oak leaves
keen back

Encumbrance

one has moved the sense
acorn
swiftly blinded kick
the fig before Charybdis

	cavernous
Coincidentia	red glow haloes upon his buttocks
Oppositorum	at lifting her hand
	the dead return
	in simple shirt

Coincidentia
Oppositorum

cavernous
red glow haloes upon his buttocks
at lifting her hand
the dead return
in simple shirt

Enumerated   myrrh egg returned to returning sun

result by which
Messenger   fine shirt
burns into his torso
elaborate day

5
from under, segmented eye, each wing
vitae, romances, letters, histories,
courtesy books

Sk'ander   chortle wind

it is as two eyes with her tear duct swollen thus

What monstrous   yellow-jacket on the yellow slide Oedipus follows
Predictor

Scale   the matter isn't what, cedar-berries

The image   what the ground cannot absorb she stands in
She constitutes
Is brought about   suddenly piercing his feet, context
In the literary   the rain is reflective so branching planar trees
Process through
The gradual revelation
Of the priority of   Sphinx, Jocasta alternating in
Paradox   similar manner alternating 0 and 1

Gives rise
To its description   one shudders at descriptor: eyebrow
                                      at predictor: brought to bear on said
                                      corner of the wall

His palm on
Her chin   fingers replace her mouth

Performa

one has, in piercing the feet so that by
hanging from the tree the boy may survive
his exposure, inclined toward the
preservation from beasts

Aristotle: for emphasis
Alexander: pumpkin
Aristotle: even so secreted
Alexander: phallus into broom

Aristotle: narrow content
Alexander: ear
Aristotle: when thus referenced
Alexander: pimple thus menacing the aural canal

A shine and black corner from the cricket

Aristotle: narrow content
Alexander: swollen, the dog's jaw, slack and sliding
Aristotle: little sores banded across buttocks, red
Alexander: from sitting to crawling
Aristotle: the nonconscious perceiving

Aristotle: like when

Alexander: there isn't any mechanism

Aristotle: shunt

Alexander: internal state one takes descriptors for

Aristotle: for which

Alexander: for which the birds aren't circling so much as
    realizing web of their own motion

Aristotle: wind over those crows

Alexander: rhinovirus

Aristotle: foot the arch

Alexander: one must possess protection as one's own skin

Aristotle: can be scaffold for emotion
Alexander: can staunch flowing blood
Aristotle: flesh
Alexander: held to flesh, a pearl

ACKNOWLEDGMENTS

Certain portions of this books first appeared in the following journals: *Fence, Colorado Review, SET, EOAGH,* and *Laurel Review* and the Black Mountain College anthology *Far from the Centers of Ambition.* I'd like to thanks the editors for their kindness.

LANCE PHILLIPS is author of three books of poetry (*Corpus Socius, Cur Aliquid Vidi* and *These Indicium Tales*) with Ahsahta Press. His poetry has also appeared in *New American Writing, Fence, Verse, Colorado Review,* and in the Black Mountain College anthology *Far from the Centers of Ambition;* it has been honored with an &Now award as well. He lives in Huntersville, North Carolina, with his wife of 20 years and their two children.

AHSAHTA PRESS

SAWTOOTH POETRY PRIZE SERIES

AHSAHTA PRESS

NEW SERIES

This book is set in Apollo MT type
with Franklin Gothic Book titles
by Ahsahta Press at Boise State University.
Cover design by Quemadura.
Book design by Janet Holmes.

AHSAHTA PRESS

2015

JANET HOLMES, DIRECTOR
ADRIAN KIEN, ASSISTANT DIRECTOR

DENISE BICKFORD

KATIE FULLER

LAURA ROGHAAR

ELIZABETH SMITH

KERRI WEBSTER